Origins

Meteorite

Chris Powling ▪ Jonatronix

D1336222

UNIVERSITY PRESS

HIGHLY CONFIDENTIAL

From: STING, Charles
To: Top secret

Subject: TEAM X

⌂ Villain profile: the Collector

To *******

Following the arrest of Dr X, we have made several changes at NICE.

- NICE is now the *National Institute for the Conservation of Earth*.
- Dani Day has been appointed to the position of Senior Scientist.
- The mission of NICE is to help protect the planet and the precious things in it.

In order to help NICE in its mission, Dani Day has employed a team of four agents. She assures me that they are highly capable. In order to protect the agents, their real identities must remain a secret. They have been given the name Team X. Their operation status is now **code green**.

Team X have been monitoring a new villain. He calls himself the Collector. The Collector is known to have carried out some serious crimes [see file attached].

I will keep you informed of any further changes.

Regards

Charles I. Sting
**Director of Operations,
NICE**

Important
Agent Information
Read this first

Villain profile: the Collector

Threat category: High

Known crimes:
- Theft of the entire population of cod in the North Atlantic.
- Theft of the White Cliffs of Dover.
- Attempted theft of the Sphinx at Giza. The robbery failed, but he did get away with the Sphinx's nose.

Appearance:
Dark hair. Brown Eyes. 182 centimetres tall. Snappy dresser. Bionic hand. Spectrum retina enhanced implant.

Profile:
The Collector is a billionaire. How he made his fortune is not known. His goal is to own the biggest collection of snow globes in the world. Using advanced micro science he shrinks and steals valuable objects. No target is too big. He does not care about the consequences of his actions.

Other things to note:
He likes to send snow globes to taunt his victims.

TEAM X DESTINATION: SAN FRANCISCO

Continent: North America
Country: United States
of America
Destination: San Francisco, California
Climate: Famous for its fog

California is known as the *Sunshine State*. The city of San Francisco is the 13th most populated city in the United States of America. It is a popular tourist destination, famous for its landmarks, including the Golden Gate Bridge and the former prison, Alcatraz.

Chapter 1 – Fireball

Victor Rodriguez gripped the edge of the rock with his fingers. With one final effort, he pulled himself up over the ridge. At last he was at the top of the mountain. He unclipped the rope from his waist and wiped the sweat from his forehead. It had been a difficult climb, but as Victor looked out over the Death Valley National Park, he knew it had been worth it.

He sat down on the rock that was still hot from the afternoon sun. He reached for his bottle of water. The temperature that day had been nearly 38 degrees, and it was still warm. Victor looked out at the dry, cracked earth and rocky horizon in front of him. The setting sun began to change the colours of the rocks from a dry biscuit yellow, to a mixture of rich gold, reds and purples. He felt the tiredness begin to seep from his aching muscles. Victor looked up and let out a long contented sigh.

Just then, the sky above him lit up in a blinding flash. He quickly got up. A bright ball of light shot across the sky above his head. It looked as though the sky was on fire.

Chapter 2 – M-35

"I'll be frank with you, Team X," said Dani Day. "Your next mission may be impossible ..." She crossed the control room of NICE headquarters and stood in front of a computer. She began to type. "Take a good long look at M-35."

Max, Cat, Ant and Tiger gathered excitedly round Dani. An image appeared on the screen. It showed a picture of an unusual object that looked like a big, metallic rock.

"A rock!" scoffed Tiger. "Is that it?"

"It's not just any old rock," said Dani.

"Is it what I think it is?" said Ant, staring hard at the screen.

"It's a meteorite," said Cat, jumping in to answer before Ant had a chance. "My dad collects them. But they are all tiny. This one looks much bigger."

"That's right," said Dani. "This one is also a bit special ..."

"I still don't see what's so great about a bit of rock," said Tiger. "Even if it is from space."

"Here," said Dani, handing Tiger a file. "Read this."

C O N F I D E N T I A L
B R I E F I N G   P A P E R

C I R C U L A T I O N :
R E S T R I C T E D   T O   S E C U R I T Y
C L E A R A N C E   C O D E   G R E E N

S U B J E C T :   M - 3 5

T O P   S E C R E T

Comets and meteorites

Definitions:

Comet

A comet is a body of ice, dust and gas that orbits the Sun. The heat from the Sun turns the outer ice into gas and the solid particles are released as dust. This forms a bright tail. The tail can be several hundred million kilometres long!

Meteoroid

A meteoroid is a piece of comet debris that orbits the Sun. Most meteroids are as small as a pebble and they burn up before they enter Earth's atmosphere.

Meteorite

A meteorite is a meteoroid that breaks through the Earth's atmosphere, does not burn up, and hits the Earth's surface.

Most meteorites have been found in Antarctica and North Africa because they are easy to find on ice and sand.

Of the many thousands of meteorites known to have landed on Earth, at least 34 are thought to have originated from the planet Mars.

M-35

The meteorite, code named M-35, was discovered in Death Valley National Park, California, USA by a climber called Victor Rodriguez.

Rodriguez gave the meteorite to the HI-SCI Institute in San Francisco. Scientists have been studying it ever since. The scientist in charge of the project is the well-known planetologist, Professor Anka.

The M-35 is a stony-iron meteorite which is a mixture of iron and stony material. It is thought to have originated from the planet Mars. It is only the 35th meteorite to come from there. It weighs 5.5 kilograms. This meteorite is not like any found before. The M-35 stores and radiates a never-ending supply of energy. **It is a powerful energy source and could help solve many of the world's energy problems.**

"Wow!" exclaimed Tiger, as he passed the file to Cat. "I can see why you're interested."

"Interested?" said Dani. "This could be one of the most important discoveries this decade."

"So what's the problem?" Max asked. "Why call Team X?"

"Ah …" said Dani. She tapped the keyboard again. The image of the M-35 vanished and in its place was a picture of a man in a crisp white lab coat. He had a halo of fluffy white hair. "This is Professor Anka. He's in charge of the M-35 project. This morning he received a package. In it was a snow globe."

"*The Collector!*" exclaimed Max.

The Collector was a master criminal with one goal – to own the biggest collection of snow globes in the world. Using advanced micro science, he was able to shrink and steal valuable objects. No target was too big for him, and he did not care about the consequences of his actions. In fact, the more mischief and mayhem he caused, the better he liked it. It was up to Team X to stop him.

"You think he wants to steal the M-35?" asked Ant.

"Exactly."

Chapter 3 – The HI-SCI Institute

Ten minutes later, Team X were ready to go.

Dani walked over to the X-gate teleport. The X-gate allowed the children to get anywhere in the world in seconds. "Professor Anka is expecting you," said Dani. "He got in touch as soon as he received the snow globe. He is looking forward to meeting you. In fact he said that the HI-SCI Institute is preparing to give you a warm welcome."

Dani typed the coordinates into the launch pad control system and the X-gate shimmered into existence.

Cat gave a little gasp. She never failed to be impressed with the X-gate teleport.

"I want you to go to the Institute and find out as much as you can about the Collector's plans," Dani said, seriously. "We must stop him stealing the M-35!"

"We'll do our best," said Max.

One by one the children leapt into the centre of the X-gate and disappeared.

Team X were standing in Professor Anka's study on the ground floor of the Institute. There were pictures and diagrams everywhere showing the M-35 from every angle. There was a cut-out made from paper, a cross-section in stainless steel and a model you could take apart like a jigsaw. While they were gazing round the room, Max noticed the professor grab something round and see-through from his desk and put it in a drawer. The professor turned and twisted his face into a smile.

"I wasn't expecting you so ... soon," said the professor. He ran a hand through his fluffy, white hair. "How did you get here so fast?"

"So much for the warm welcome!" Tiger whispered to Ant.

"NICE have always been quick off the mark," Max said, briskly. "I'm Max, Professor. And this is Cat, Ant and Tiger. Dani Day sent us."

"Yes," said the professor, looking them up and down. "I only wish I could find a good use for you," he said, waving his hand as if brushing away a fly.

"What do you mean?" asked Cat, who didn't

like the professor's tone one bit.

"I mean, I'm afraid you've had a wasted journey."

"But what about the Collector?" burst out Ant. "Aren't you worried about the M-35?"

"Yeah, you called NICE remember?" said Tiger, grumpily.

"I fear I overreacted a bit this morning," said the professor. "I've realized that everything that can be done is being done. We have upgraded all our security systems. I really don't see how the Collector can steal the M-35."

"You don't know him," Tiger warned. "He's very clever, you know."

"So am I," said the professor pointedly. "I have three degrees and so many other qualifications, I've lost count."

"Still, the Collector has got past security systems before," said Max.

"But nothing like this!" replied the professor. "We have the most hi-tech security system in the world. Let me show you."

The professor led the children out of his office and down the corridor. He stopped outside a large metal door. "Look," he said, punching a code into the keypad.

Ant's mouth dropped open as he stared round the room. The M-35 was protected by the most advanced security system he had ever come across.

"There is a computerized lock with a code that changes every hour," boasted the professor. "There are pressure sensors on the floor and around the edges of the room. There is a web of laser beams that a spider would have problems getting through. And there are motion sensors sweeping the room. Plus we have 24-hour security guards. No expense has been spared. The set-up here is state-of-the-art!"

The professor pushed a button and the door to the room slammed tightly shut.

"So you see, nothing can get in or out without being detected."

"Bet we could," sniffed Tiger.

"Tiger!" warned Max, quietly. "You mean there's nothing we can do to help, Professor?"

"Not a thing."

"So what do we do now?" asked Cat.

"You could go home," said Professor Anka. "Or you could have a holiday. California is called the *Sunshine State*, you know."

Chapter 4 – Tiger's idea

Max, Cat, Ant and Tiger made their way down to the beach. It was shrouded in fog.

"Sunshine State indeed!" snorted Tiger.

Cat scuffed up some sand with her trainer.

"Holiday!" she said, furiously. "Is that all he thinks of Team X?"

"Looks like it," said Max, staring at the ground. "He certainly has more faith in those alarms and lasers than he does in us."

"They were pretty impressive," admitted Ant.

"They won't stop the Collector," snapped Tiger. "The professor has no idea how cunning he is." Frustrated, he kicked at a stone.

"So what happens now?" asked Cat.

Just then, the fog began to lift as the sun broke through. The children glimpsed a beach that seemed to go on forever. The windows of the HI-SCI Institute glittered brightly in the distance.

"It's obvious," Tiger said. "We've got to prove to the professor that his security system is not unbreakable."

"That's it, Tiger!" exclaimed Ant. "If *we* can get to the M-35, Professor Anka will have to take us seriously."

Chapter 5 – Security breach

Team X spent the rest of the day planning how they would get to the M-35. Max contacted Dani via his holographic watch and asked her to send some equipment through the X-gate, including the mole-shaped X-craft – the Driller. Ant managed to download a map of the HI-SCI Institute on to a laptop that Dani sent him. Then, they went over and over their plan until it seemed perfect. Surely nothing could go wrong?

Late in the evening, Max, Cat, Ant and Tiger crept up to the HI-SCI Institute.

"Well, the professor was right about the security guards," said Cat, looking through the glass doors. A man in a uniform was pacing up and down.

"Come on," said Max, leading them round the side of the building.

When they were safely hidden in the shadows, Max shrugged off his rucksack. He carefully lifted out the Driller and put it on the ground. As he did so, he made the others repeat the first part of the plan they had rehearsed.

"Perfect!" grinned Max, when they had finished. "Ready to shrink?"

They turned the dials on their special watches anticlockwise. A bright blue X appeared in the centre of each one. They pushed the X and, in an instant, the team were micro-sized. Max pushed another button on his watch and a door on the side of the Driller slid open with a hiss. They all climbed inside.

Tiger took the controls. "Let's go!" he said, switching on the engine.

The Driller rumbled into life. Tiger pushed a lever and it jerked forwards.

"Tiger!" yelped Cat, who had nearly fallen out of her seat. She quickly strapped herself in.

"Sorry!" Tiger said. "Haven't driven for a while."

"Let's go, Tiger," said Max.

Tiger pushed a lever forwards and the Driller began to dig down into the ground with its huge metal claws.

The smell of earth and grit drifted through the air vents. Progress was slow, but when they had reached the bottom of the building, Tiger levelled out the craft.

"Right," he said. "Which way?"

Ant flipped up the screen of his laptop and looked at the plan of the HI-SCI building. Cat used the compass on her watch and, together, they guided Tiger towards the M-35.

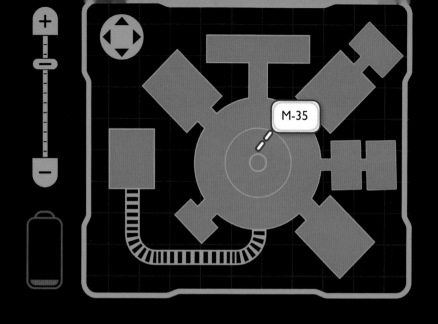

"So," said Cat, recapping, "we bypass the door lock and come up in the M-35 room, then disable the pressure sensors?"

"Correct," said Max.

As they got nearer to the M-35 however, the light on Ant's laptop began to flash.

"Oh, no!" he exclaimed. "The battery is running low. We don't have much time."

"Try to memorize the route," said Max. But even as he was talking, the whirring of the computer stopped and the laptop switched itself off.

"Which way?" said Tiger, trying to hold the juddering machine in a straight line.

Ant closed his eyes. "I think ..." he said, desperately trying to hold the image from the screen in his mind. "North west."

Tiger turned the Driller. After a few minutes, Ant told Tiger to start digging up.

"Are you sure?" said Cat, looking worried.

"It's my best guess," shrugged Ant.

"Good enough for me," said Max. "Take us up, Tiger."

Unfortunately, the Driller did not come up in the M-35 room as planned. They surfaced in the corridor on the wrong side of the steel doors. Tiger switched off the engine.

"Can't we just dig back down?" said Cat.

Max checked his watch. "No time. Don't worry, Ant," he said, noticing his friend looked upset. "We'll just need you to get us past that lock instead." He pointed up to a control panel by the side of the steel doors.

Ant smiled at Max. "Just the kind of challenge I like," he said.

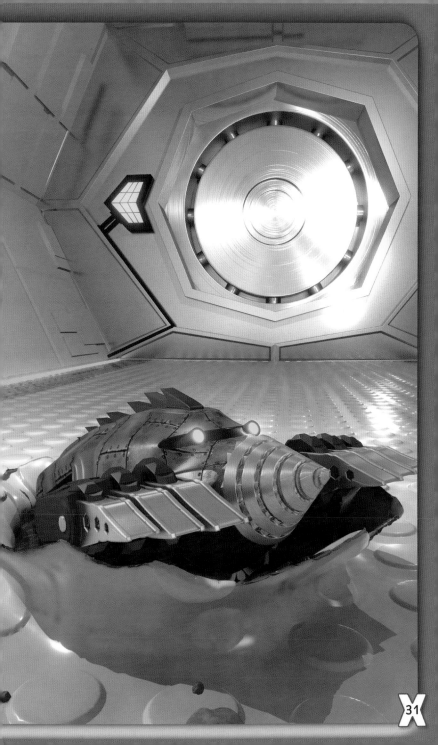

Team X climbed out of the Driller and discussed what to do. They knew that they should not return to normal size. They had a much better chance of remaining hidden from the security cameras if they were micro-sized. But that left the problem of reaching the computerized lock. Ant was not a great climber, but he was the best one for the job. Max decided that they would have to winch Ant up.

Cat got out a rope, harness and a portable u-shaped hook from the Driller's equipment box. Tiger made easy work of reaching the computerized lock by scrambling up the electric cable that powered it. He secured the hook to the wall and threaded the rope through. Then he climbed down. Max, Cat and Tiger pulled the rope and hoisted Ant up. He had always hated heights, so he didn't look down.

When he was level with keypad Ant set to work. He had read about this type of lock on the Internet. It was a prime number lock – the code used numbers that were only divisible by themselves. He just needed the right combination of numbers.

Ant began to type and, after a while, the door was open. Ant heard a small cheer from below. Max, Cat and Tiger lowered Ant to the floor and they quickly ran into the room. The door slammed shut behind them. They could see the M-35 on its stand in the middle of the room. Red lasers criss-crossed in front of it and the blue motion-sensor beams swept the room at intervals.

"Easy!" laughed Tiger, nervously.

"One thing at a time," said Max.

"What about the pressure sensors on the floor?" said Cat.

"As we're micro-size," said Ant. "We may just be able to cross them. But no falling over!"

They had to go one by one. Max went first. He held his breath as he ran lightly over the pad. It was like walking on a giant cushion and was difficult to keep upright. But somehow he managed it. He beckoned the others to follow.

Then they made their way across the rest of the room: ducking, dodging and rolling away from motion sensors, crawling under and jumping over laser beams.

It was like an extreme assault course. Finally they made it to the middle of the room. They turned the dials on their watches clockwise. In an instant, the team were back to normal size. They stood in front of the dome that housed the meteorite.

"The M-35," gasped Cat.

Max, Cat, Ant and Tiger circled around it like bees around a honey pot. The meteorite was almost within their grasp. All they had to do was lift the dome in the way Ant had shown them and ...

"Well done, Team!" said Max. "Professor Anka will have to take us seriously now."

"Wait ..." said Ant, suddenly.

"What's wrong?" asked Cat.

Ant was staring at the M-35. He took off his glasses and rubbed them on his sleeve. When they were back on his nose, he stared even harder. "Something's wrong all right," he whispered, touching the meteorite's surface. "Take a good look for yourselves. This isn't the M-35 at all. What we've got here is a *fake!*"

Chapter 6 – The fake

"A fake?" Cat gasped.

"How can it be a fake?" demanded Tiger.

"Because it's made from plastic," Ant groaned. "The real meteorite is stone and iron."

Max picked it up. It was far too light to be the real M-35. It also felt warm, not cold like stone. "Ant's right," he said at last. "It's a plastic copy. It's cleverly put together but still a copy."

Just then, they heard the door to the room open again. Standing there was Professor Anka. He started clapping.

"Oh, well done, Team X," he said, sarcastically. "Well done indeed."

"Professor?" said Cat. "What's going on?"

"Isn't it obvious?" said Ant. "The M-35 is not the only fake in the room."

The professor started to laugh. He reached up to his neck and began to peel the skin back.

"Oh, gross!" winced Cat, as the false professor pulled off his mask.

"The Collector," growled Max.

"So, where's the M-35?" asked Ant.

"And where's your Master-bot?" snorted Tiger. "Don't you normally send that to do your dirty work for you?"

"My Master-bot, as you call it," said the Collector, glaring at them. "Is on another little errand for me. Besides, I'd always wanted a trip to California. As for the M-35, it's already been shrunk to micro-size and is safely in a snow globe." He gave a short manic laugh.

Max thought back to when they had been in the study. He remembered seeing the fake professor putting something in his drawer.

"Where's the real professor?" he asked.

"You'll soon find out," said the Collector. He reached towards a button on the side of the wall. "You see, I told you this place had the most advanced security system around." Then he pushed the button and a trap door opened underneath Team X. Screaming, they all fell into the darkness.

Team X landed with a thump at the bottom of the chute.

"Ouch," said Cat, as she thumped on to the floor.

Max was already up. "Everyone all right?" he asked, dusting himself down. Thankfully no one was hurt.

"Who on earth are you?" said a voice, from the shadows on the other side of the room.

The children all jumped. They turned to see a man in a crisp white lab coat. He had a halo of fluffy white hair.

"Professor Anka?" asked Cat, suspiciously.

"That's me," said the real professor.

"Are you sure?" said Tiger. "Only we've been fooled once today."

"Of course I'm sure. But you still haven't answered my question ... who are you?"

"Sorry, Professor," said Max, quickly. "We're from NICE."

"Dani Day sent us to help!" Cat added.

The professor raised his eyebrows. "Help?" he said, as he looked around the sealed room – there was no way out.

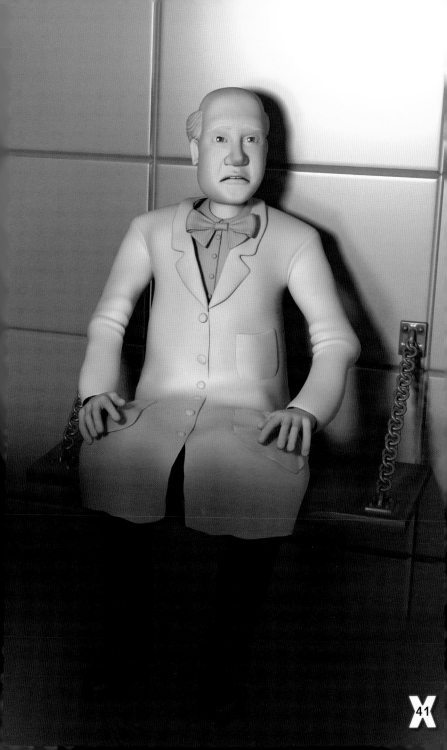

Chapter 7 — Escape!

"It seems we've all fallen for the Collector's cunning plan," said the professor.

Tiger looked at the steep chute they had all just tumbled out of. "Fallen! Ha, I get it. Nice one, Professor."

The professor looked at him oddly.

To break the awkward silence that followed, Max explained how they had been duped by the Collector. The professor then told them how he had been fooled by one of the Collector's disguises, too – a security expert – and how he had been trapped in a similar way to Team X.

"So how are we going to get out?" asked Cat.

"You can't get out … not out of here," said the professor miserably.

"Time for a meeting, Team," said Max. "Excuse us, Professor."

Max gathered Cat, Ant and Tiger round him in the far corner of the room. "It's not just escaping," he said. "We need to get the M-35 back before the Collector disappears."

"Any ideas?" asked Tiger.

"Just one," Max said.

He explained his plan to the others. He reminded them how his watch could activate the Driller remotely. They could set the homing control to synchronize with the tracking function on Cat's watch. Once they had the Driller back, they could then go after the M-35.

"Great plan," said Tiger.

The others agreed. Two minutes later, after typing in some instructions on the screen of his watch, Max had tapped into the Driller's remote control circuits. Cat tracked the silver dot on her watch. Their craft was on its way.

"Err, I've just thought of one small snag," Ant said. "The laptop is still down. We don't have a plan of the building. So how will we find our way round when we're underground?"

Max looked over his shoulder at the professor.

"We can't take him with us!" gasped Tiger. "He can't shrink! Besides, you know the rules … we can't tell anyone about our watches."

"Let me handle it," said Max. He walked over to the professor. "Professor, we need you to trust Team X. We've thought of a way out and how to save the meteorite."

"Tell me!"

"That's where the trust comes in, Professor," Max said. "You see, it's top secret."

Max asked the professor to draw a map of the building in the dust on the floor. He wanted to know exactly where they were and where the professor's study was. He then got Ant to take a photo of the dust map with his watch so he didn't need to remember it.

Just as they finished, they heard a rumbling in the floor underneath them.

"Now, Professor," said Max. "I'm going to have to ask you to turn around and face the wall."

"Why?" demanded the professor.

"We will get your meteorite back and we will get you out of here," Max continued. "That's a promise, Professor."

Professor Anka sighed and turned away.

At that moment the Driller burst up through the floor.

"Ready?" asked Max.

"Ready," said Cat, Ant and Tiger together.

They all turned their watches anticlockwise.

Once again Team X were back in their craft and burrowing down.

"Full power, Tiger," said Max. "We don't have much time. I only hope the snow globe is still there."

Using the photograph of the map, they tunnelled their way under the building towards the professor's study. Soon they were digging their way upwards again.

"Let's just hope we get it right this time," said Ant.

They broke through the surface. The carpet on the floor of the office muffled the noise of the drill.

"Perfect!" said Max.

"Where are we?" said Cat.

"Right underneath the professor's desk! The M-35 snow globe is directly above us."

Under directions from Max, Tiger burrowed straight up into the bottom of the drawer.

"Quick," said Cat, straining to hear above the noise of splintering wood. "I can hear footsteps."

A hole had appeared in the bottom of the drawer.

"The snow globe," shouted Ant, "there it is!"

"Stop drilling!" ordered Max.

Tiger hit a button and the drill slowed to a stop just as the door swung open. The Collector burst into the room.

"Time I was on the move," muttered the Collector to himself.

"Release the grappling arm, quick!" said Max.

Tiger pulled a series of levers and the nose of the drill opened up. A grappling hook extended out. It gripped the base of the snow globe and Tiger reeled it in tight.

They could hear the Collector coming round to the back of the desk.

"Reverse!" shouted Max.

Tiger pulled on another lever. At once, the Driller together with the snow globe containing the M-35 backed down into the hole.

From deep inside the tunnel, the children could hear the screams of the Collector above them.

"WHERE'S MY SNOW GLOBE?" his voice echoed. "WHERE'S MY METEORITE?"

Back at NICE HQ ...

Team X had just finished retelling their story to Dani.

"It's a shame the Collector escaped," said Dani.

"Yes," said Max, glumly. "By the time we released the professor and alerted the security guards, he'd disappeared."

"Cheer up, Max," replied Dani. "The most important thing is that you saved the M-35."

"After we had returned it to its normal size we gave it back to the professor," explained Ant.

"What's going to happen to it now?" asked Cat.

"The professor said it will be removed to a location that really is top secret. Then it can be studied in peace," explained Dani.

"So, it seems our mission was not so impossible after all," laughed Tiger.